The Proven Method For **Potty Training &** Fostering **Independence**

The Proven Method For **Potty Training &** Fostering **Independence**

Dr. Deanna Mason

The Proven Method for Potty Training and Fostering Independence

www.proactiveparenting.com

Edition & design: Audiskills.com
Layout: www.produccioneditorial.com
ISBN: 978-84-129271-3-9

Contents

Introduction

Hi there! Welcome to my book *The Proven Method for Potty Training and Fostering Independence*. I'm Doctor Deanna Mason, and in the following lessons, I'll share the key steps to help your little one develop the skills to become more independent in their daily activities, personal care, and that one issue that concerns many parents: toilet training.

Culturally, there's often a sense of competition among parents to see whose child reaches certain milestones first—whether it's crawling, walking, eating without a fuss, or, of course, getting out of diapers. But the truth is, this kind of competition is pointless because each child develops at their own unique pace. What matters isn't if a child does something before or after another, but rather that they do it when they're ready.

In this book, we're going to look the issue of our little one's independence. The challenge with this subject is that there are no absolute rules about when or how much we should intervene in this process. It might sound tricky, but it really isn't. The secret is that, for the most part, your child will set the pace for what they want and are able to do. Your job will be to respond to their natural developmental process by creating appropriate boundaries.

Encouraging Autonomy from an Early Age

I once worked with a family with two young daughters, ages 5 and 3. When the parents got divorced, they started doing everything for the girls—bathing them, dressing them, taking them to the bathroom, picking up their toys, feeding them, and even pushing them in strollers so they wouldn't get tired.

It wasn't until the girls' school brought it up that the parents realized they were holding their daughters back from learning to care for themselves. They had to make some changes and start involving the girls in everyday tasks. At first, it wasn't easy, and the girls resisted. But with patience and persistence, a year later, the girls were more independent, had better self-control, and were happier because they felt more confident in their abilities. Even their parents were amazed at what they could do!

In this case, the development of essential skills was delayed because the parents underestimated what their daughters were capable of. Whether it was to make the girls feel more loved or because it was simply easier for the parents, by not allowing the girls some responsibility for their own care, they missed out on learning and practicing fundamental life skills.

Every Child Has Their Own Pace

When children are allowed to do more and more things for themselves and gradually get better at them, it creates a snowball effect that motivates them to continue learning.

On the other hand, some parents have expectations that are too high for what their child can realistically do. This could mean they expect their child to master a skill almost overnight or push them to take steps they aren't ready for.

A common example of this is potty training. I've worked with many families where the process of learning to use the toilet became stressful because the parents were convinced it was time to ditch the diapers, even though the child wasn't showing signs of readiness. Just like with other milestones, it's the child who will give clear signals when they're ready to learn a new skill. So, how can we approach this in the best way?

Prevention Over Correction

My *Proactive Parenting Method* provides an answer. It focuses on prevention rather than correction. In order for it to work, those in charge of a child's upbringing need to understand their child's development. This way of raising children helps identify potentially problematic situations early on, neutralizing them before they become more difficult to manage. The goal is to anticipate behaviors so you can guide your child more consciously toward desired outcomes.

I developed this method based on my 30 years of experience working with children. I studied Registered nursing in the United States, my home country, where I also became a certified Nurse Practitioner. I was always fascinated by the parent-child relationship and the common issues that arise, so I specialized in Pediatrics and later earned a PhD in Nursing, where I developed this method. My work in hospitals, clinics, schools, and universities in both the U.S. and Spain has informed my method, as well as extensive qualitative research. I now spend my time helping parents like you raise their children with an approach supported by science.

Thinking Long-Term

The information I share is designed to give parents clear and useful insights into what science tells us about child development. My aim to explain that, physically, mentally, and emotionally, every child needs to go through a series of steps to develop properly.

With that in mind, this method takes a long-term view. The steps you take today in parenting, no matter how big or small, will lead to future successes for both you and your child. That's why it's better to focus on building behaviors that prioritize your child's well-being and safety, helping them become more independent over time. This way, you can maximize their potential as they grow.

Proactive parenting is flexible—it adapts to the unique values and context of each family. It offers parents the tools they need to confidently and lovingly guide their children through every stage of development. One of the great benefits of this method is that it strengthens parent-child bonds, leading to a happier, more harmonious family life. Sounds pretty good, right?

For Parents of Toddlers and Preschoolers

This course is designed for parents of children between 12 months and five years of age—those who are raising little ones experiencing many things for the first time. This is a crucial period for teaching our kiddos basic skills, setting limits to prevent problematic behaviors, and guiding them toward desired attitudes.

I can't emphasize enough how important it is for parents to be observant of their child's development. Every child is different. So, while I can share general guidelines with you, it's your child who will let you know whether they're ready to move forward or if they need more time. Keeping this in mind will help you set realistic expectations for what your child can achieve, which will prevent frustration for both of you. Understanding your child better will also allow you to support them more effectively, making them feel more secure.

There's a quote by Denis Waitley that I love, and find particularly fitting for this course: "The best gifts you can give your children are the roots of responsibility and the wings of independence." In other words, if we teach our children the importance of limits, discipline, and responsibility, they will grow up with the tools they need to become self-reliant and responsible adults who feel loved and supported. Isn't that the best thing we can do for them?

Building Confidence and Independence

Over the next four lessons, you'll learn the foundations for helping your child develop physical autonomy with confidence, safety, and appropriate boundaries. You'll get tools to establish appropriate limits, help your child feel secure as they learn new physical skills, guide them through the potty-training process, and involve them in their personal care. If you apply these strategies, I guarantee your child will enter the next phase of their life feeling capable and with a sense of self-confidence that supports their self-esteem.

Let's get started.

Lesson 1

Setting Boundaries with a Proactive Parenting Approach

As I mentioned earlier, the foundation of Proactive Parenting is focusing on prevention rather than correction. This is especially true when it comes to setting boundaries for our children. We all worry about their safety. Unlike other species, humans depend on their parents from birth and throughout the early years of life. It's our responsibility to protect our kids until they can take care of themselves.

However, no baby comes with an instruction manual. What they do have is a natural drive to explore their environment and try new things. This is where one of the biggest challenges of parenting comes in: How do you protect them, and how much? How much freedom should you give them, and at what point? When should you step back, and when should you intervene?

The truth is, there's no single right answer to these questions. But the good news is, there are ways to make this process easier for both you and your child.

Contextual Limits

Let's consider two scenarios. In the first, a three-year-old is brought to visit their aunt and uncle. The parents sit down to chat with their hosts, letting the child roam freely. Believing the house is safe, they stop paying attention. At one point, the child reaches for an object on a high shelf, knocking it over and breaking it. The parents only react after hearing the crash and their child's cry.

In the second scenario, a family attends a formal dinner. The parents force their two-year-old to sit still with them, hoping the child will stay occupied with the toys they brought. When the child gets restless and tries to move or get their parents' attention, the scolding begins: "Sit still," "Don't touch that," "Stop yelling."

Both situations highlight boundaries that don't fit the child's age or context. In the first case, too much freedom without supervision led to an accident. In the second, the child is likely frustrated because they're being asked to behave in a way that's unnatural for their age.

The solution can be as simple or as complex as establishing limits that ensure your child's safety without stifling their natural learning experiences. It's essential to create a structure of boundaries that protect your child. Let's look at how to use the principles of Proactive Parenting to foster your child's growth and development while prioritizing their safety. Although this approach applies to physical, emotional and social safety, in this course, we'll focus on physical safety.

The Proactive Parenting Model

Imagine three concentric circles, each within the other.

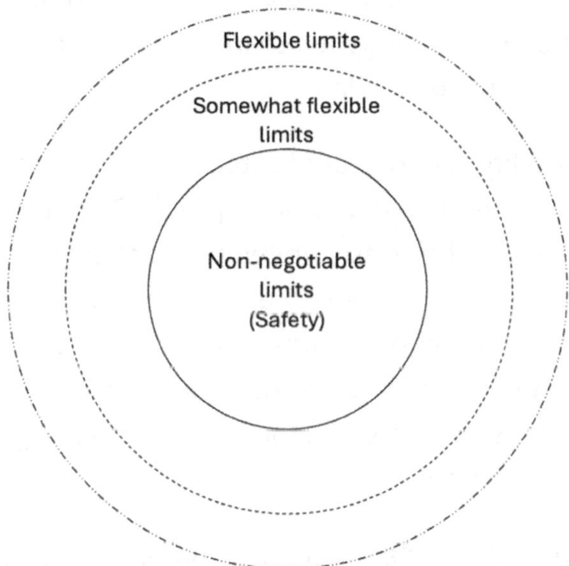

The solid line represents non-negotiable limits, the dashed line indicates slightly flexible limits, and the dotted line represents flexible limits.

The innermost circle represents your child's safety—these are the non-negotiable boundaries. These cover situations where your child could put themselves in danger, so you must intervene to protect them. To help your child understand these limits, you'll need to explain that your interventions aren't just arbitrary—they're part of your role in keeping them safe.

The middle circle encompasses things related to your family's values and routines, like mealtimes, sleep, or manners. These limits are important but allow some flexibility depending on the context. For example, eating and sleeping well are crucial, so they have set routines. However, during a visit to the grandparents, it might be okay to let your child have a cookie before dinner or stay up a bit later.

This flexibility is important for teaching children that life is complex and often unpredictable. While it's essential to be consistent when teaching values and routines, the aim is to maintain the rules about 80% of the time and allow exceptions around 20% of the time. This balance helps your child learn the expectations while also adapting to small changes in their environment.

The outermost circle covers boundaries related to values that are less critical to your family but that you still want your child to learn. These are usually situations where children learn through the natural consequences of not following the boundaries.

For example, let's say your 4-year-old doesn't want to put on their shoes to go to the park and asks you to do it for them. You might set the expectation like this: "We need to put on our shoes before we can go to the park," and give them time to comply. If they take too long, explain that it's now too late to go. Encourage them to try again tomorrow. This way, they learn that their actions have consequences, and it encourages positive behavior changes.

This outer circle is great for teaching your child about their responsibilities, rights, and the natural consequences of their choices. And trust me, these lessons will come in handy when they reach their teenage years—it's never too early to start!

The size of these circles will change as your child grows and develops. In the first year, children want to explore everything, but they don't yet understand what is safe or unsafe, and they rely on you to guide them. That's why, in the first 12 months, the inner circle occupies nearly all the space. The middle circle allows for some simple structures and boundaries, like introducing new foods or learning table manners. The outer circle, at this stage, is nearly nonexistent since toddlers are too young to take any risks that could harm their well-being. However, it's still relevant for developing habits and learning from natural consequences.

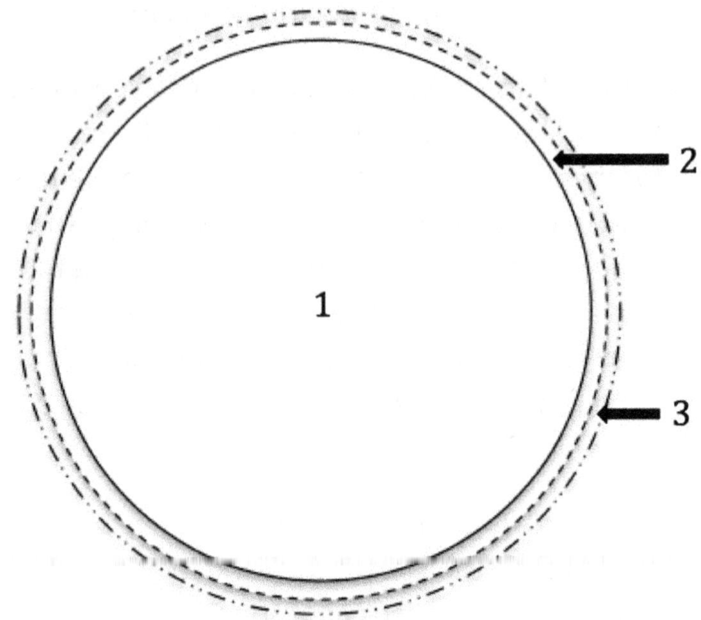

For a 12-month-old, the inner circle of non-negotiable limits takes up almost all the space.

Increasing Flexibility

As your child grows, the areas of flexibility in both the middle and outer circles expand. By the time they're about 4 years old, they'll have a greater understanding of their surroundings, and they'll have learned the family's expectations and boundaries. By this age, your child should be able to follow instructions and distinguish right from wrong in situations that may affect their safety. This is the time when they'll learn new rules and limits to navigate more complex situations. However, always remember that they still lack experience and will continue to need your supervision to stay safe.

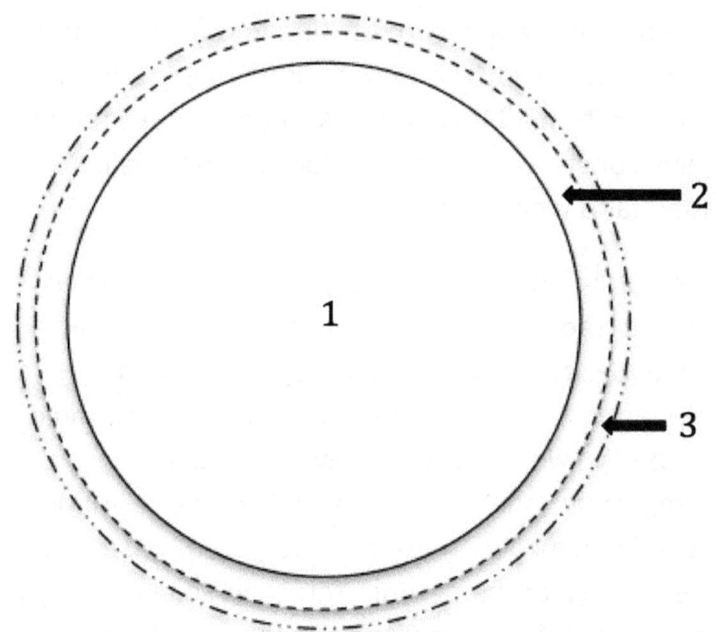

For a 4-year-old, the area of non-negotiable limits takes up the majority, but there is still room for moderately flexible and flexible limits.

Eventually, the outer circle will expand further, especially as your child faces situations that require them to make decisions, such as choosing to be kind or rough when playing. The natural consequences of their choices will motivate them to repeat or adjust their behavior.

Repetition and Patience

Children learn new behaviors through repetition, which allows them to practice skills. Although this is more obvious in physical activities, like walking, the same principle applies to learning about behavior. As parents, we need to be patient and understand that we won't see immediate results. We need to take the time to give consistent and clear information to help them understand what we expect.

Be mindful if your child starts to challenge you when they hear the word "no" or when asked to stop doing something. It's important that they understand these are expectations for their safety, not a game. To reinforce this, use the word "no" sparingly but consistently, only for important moments. "No" should carry weight but be used minimally. For lesser issues, use phrases like "listen," "hey," or "be careful." You can also reinforce your message with facial expressions, tone of voice, or by gently moving them away from a dangerous situation.

Safety Begins with Boundaries

Establishing a firm framework with clear boundaries is the most effective way to protect your child as they grow. It's not about stopping them from doing things out of fear of injury, but rather giving them the opportunity to try age-appropriate activities while ensuring their safety.

Increased Vigilance in Early Years

I emphasize physical safety so much because, during the first five years, children aren't yet capable of thinking through the consequences of their actions. They are often so focused on exploring their surroundings that they could put themselves at risk—like running after a ball into the street, putting objects in their mouths, or falling while trying to reach something.

The goal, in the medium and long term, is to help your child develop a clear understanding of consequences so that they learn to protect themselves, even when you're not around. They'll not only be safe but grow up confident that they can make the right decisions because they've been given a solid foundation for choosing the right actions.

Teaching children about boundaries also helps them learn self-regulation. A big part of this process is understanding that their actions have consequences, both for themselves and those around them. This is the foundation of self-control.

Practicing Limits in Everyday Situations

There are many situations outside the home where clear boundaries are necessary. What behaviors can we reasonably expect?

On the street: Teach your child to always hold an adult's hand and stay on the sidewalk.

In a parking lot: While loading groceries, instruct your child to stay close to the car or have them get in their seat and fasten their seatbelt.

There are certain environments where, regardless of how well your child behaves, it's unrealistic to expect them to stay still for long periods. In these cases, it's essential to be mindful and set realistic expectations for their behavior—especially when they may become bored or tired. You'll need to be more attuned to their needs in these situations.

While it's reasonable to ask them to be stay still, we also can't forget that they are still children. Think about it like this: a good rule of thumb for attention span is about 5 to 10 minutes for every year of age. So, for a child between 12 and 24 months, you can expect them to stay still for around 10 minutes before they'll want to move, explore, or get your attention. Don't expect a toddler to sit quietly through a two-hour dinner.

Of course, these guidelines can vary depending on where you live and your specific context. The key is to understand that there are different rules you can teach your child to follow, but those rules must be appropriate to their developmental stage.

Putting It into Practice

Once your child turns one, it's a great time to start defining the essential rules that will guide your parenting. This is the moment to establish a daily structure of limits and put it into practice.

Start with behaviors your child can reasonably follow at various stages, helping them learn how to stay safe. You can use the examples from this lesson or adapt them to fit your unique context. I recommend jotting down these rules in a notebook to keep them clear—and start applying them right away!

In the next section, we'll dive deeper into the natural learning process by age, giving you greater clarity on what you can expect.

Lesson 2

Developing Physical Independence

A couple had a very active three-year-old son named Alan, who loved physical activities. As soon as he could walk, his father encouraged him to engage in all sorts of physical challenges. At the park, he would help Alan climb structures he couldn't reach on his own, help him tackle obstacles that were advanced for his age, and frequently told him to ignore his fear of heights.

Alan's father believed that by always being there to catch him, he was helping build his son's confidence. Alan's mother, however, was more anxious about their son's impulsiveness. She felt like she couldn't take her eyes off him for a second, worried he might get hurt. On the way to the park, Alan would often take off running without paying attention to his surroundings, completely ignoring his mother's calls to stop.

As the mother's concern grew, Alan's father dismissed it as typical behavior for his age—until one day, Alan climbed onto equipment meant for older kids. He didn't stop when his mother called out, realizing too late that he was beyond her reach. He kept climbing higher until, suddenly terrified, he began crying for his mother to help him.

Understanding Your Child's Natural Development

While his mother was making her way to him, Alan lost his balance and fell face-first onto the sand. His mother felt incredibly guilty for not preventing the fall, though fortunately, no serious harm was done.

Alan's father was shocked that Alan hadn't listened to his mother or been scared while climbing. But Alan had learned from his father that there were no limits to what he could do—someone would always be there to keep him safe. This is a common situation: with the best intentions, parents can sometimes push their children into situations they're not yet ready for. Certain activities, games, and tools are designed for specific age ranges, respecting a child's natural physical and mental development. Even if some kids start doing things earlier, there's a developmental range we shouldn't ignore.

In Alan's case, the logical thought should have been: if he can't reach the equipment to get up on his own, he won't be able to get down either. So why put him there in the first place? A three-year-old is too young to understand that something isn't appropriate for their age—especially if their parents are the ones putting them in that situation. The message Alan received was that, regardless of his physical ability, there was always a way to bypass those limits. However, just because a child can physically manage certain things, it doesn't mean they are ready for them.

Encouraging Independence and Resilience

We've already discussed the importance of setting boundaries and understanding a child's natural development. When it comes to learning physical independence, parents often fall into one of two extremes: either pushing their child to do things beyond their ability or doing everything for them.

The latter is also quite common. Parents often step in too quickly when they see their child struggling with something. But if this becomes a habit, they may be hindering their child's physical development. Children will quickly learn that if they can't succeed right away, their parents will step in—or they might decide they simply don't want to try at all.

Instead, parents should allow their child to experience frustration when they can't complete a new task. Offer support, yes, but don't do it for them. Take a simple example: a toy where the child has to fit shapes into the correct holes. This activity is crucial for brain development and helps build skills like using scissors in the future. The child needs to repeat the action until they master it. But many parents, when they see their child failing several times, will do it for them.

Supporting Without Overstepping

The right approach is to let the child try until they succeed—encourage them, tell them they can do it, and urge them to keep trying. It's essential for children to know their parents are there to support them. This builds the child's confidence, knowing they can rely on their parents for encouragement while learning to do things independently. It may seem simple, but this is key to developing resilience and frustration tolerance. Gradually, they'll start doing more and more on their own as part of their development. Trust your child and their ability to progress!

Parents may not always realize how important this is or how much influence they have on their child's life. But it's crucial to let children try, fail, and try again, as many times as needed, while providing emotional support during moments of frustration. Understanding a child's natural learning process and knowing what they're capable of at each age is essential for healthy development.

Another common example is when parents continue using bottles well into a child's third year because it's easier and more convenient—no spills, no mess. However, sticking with the bottle for too long can hinder the development of other important skills. A child can begin using a plastic cup as early as 9 or 10 months. Start by letting them play with the cup to get familiar, and then introduce small amounts of water. With regular practice, most children master using a cup by 12 to 14 months.

Building Everyday Life Skills

A similar situation arises when children are learning to use utensils. The temptation to intervene when they spill food is strong, but it's important to let them practice feeding themselves. While toddlers have decent hand-eye coordination, they may not have the dexterity to handle a spoon or fork perfectly. Provide child-sized utensils for them to practice, but also let them eat with their hands. Over time, they'll imitate adults and gradually get the hang of it. Dirty faces and hands can always be cleaned up later!

Putting these lessons into practice requires enough time for the child to develop new habits. The best place to start is at home, in a relaxed environment where there's no pressure, and a little mess won't matter. Trying this for the first time in a restaurant might not be the best idea, but why not designate a day at home to work on these skills?

Parents don't intervene only for convenience—sometimes it's out of fear. Many parents believe that by doing everything for their children, they're keeping them safe. But this can have the opposite effect. Beyond hindering development, it deprives your child of valuable lessons about safety and problem-solving.

Assessing Risks

Learning physical independence goes hand-in-hand with safety. The goal is to measure risks to prevent injury while still allowing children to develop new skills. This is the most effective way to guide them toward independence safely. It's about prevention while keeping your child actively involved.

That said, we must acknowledge that injuries are the leading cause of death and illness after a child's first birthday. However, many risks, such as poisoning, falls, drowning, burns, and fires, are preventable. That's why it's essential to supervise children closely and teach them to recognize and respect boundaries.

Identifying Potential Hazards

The first step is learning to recognize potential dangers. As children develop new skills, they gain access to more things and activities. The key is to anticipate what they might attempt and put preventive measures in place to ensure their safety. There's a clear relationship between developmental milestones, expected behaviors, potential risks, and preventive strategies.

Starting with the basics: very young children should never be left unsupervised. They don't yet have the judgment to discern what's safe or dangerous. They act on impulse, driven by the desire to explore the world around them, so the only way to keep them safe is to control where they go and what they do.

As they grow and their curiosity increases, there are a number of safety precautions to take. When children begin to move around, you should secure doors and windows, block off stairs, keep cleaning products and chemicals out of reach, cover electrical outlets, and use safety locks on drawers and cabinets. You'll also need to limit access to dangerous areas like the bathroom, kitchen, tool sheds or pools.

Extra Precaution During the Early Stages

When children start running, climbing, or riding bikes, watch out for falls, sunburns, and ensure that outdoor play areas are safe from traffic. During the early years, you also need to watch they don't put things in their mouths. Apart from harmful substances, always check the play area for small objects that could cause choking. Be mindful of certain foods like grapes, hot dogs, and cherries, which should be cut into quarters to avoid choking hazards. And it's always best to supervise mealtimes.

If your child has siblings or cousins close in age, or is starting school, rough play can sometimes lead to bumps and scratches. It's best to supervise and intervene if any harmful behavior arises.

Age-Appropriate Guidelines

Here are some general safety guidelines to follow as your child grows:

12 to 15 months: Your child will want to explore their surroundings. If possible, create a safe area where they can play and you can supervise, while you go about your tasks. During this stage, it's crucial to praise your child when they listen to your instructions. Positive reinforcement of good behavior will encourage them to repeat it. Celebrate their successes to promote healthy, positive behaviors.

16 to 24 months: As physical abilities increase; children still have very limited impulse control. During this stage, it's essential to continue supervising their safety, from securing furniture to monitoring access to rooms. Even though they're older, it's important to speak with them consistently about how to stay safe—be patient but firm. Also, don't forget to praise them when they manage to control their impulses, like resisting the urge to run toward a busy street or a pool.

24 months to 3 years: One of the biggest dangers during this stage is what we call "magical thinking," where children believe things can happen just because they wish for them. As a result, they may try to imitate something impossible that they've seen on TV. At this stage, they still need close supervision, especially if they've been quiet for too long—always check what they're up to!

4 to 5 years: At this age, your child is starting to develop a more realistic understanding of the world. They've had plenty of practice with limits and rules, though they may still struggle to predict the outcomes of their actions. Fortunately, their language skills have developed, so you can explain the consequences of their choices more effectively.

5 to 6 years: By the time your child reaches this age, you'll begin to see the results of your hard work. If you've been consistent, your child will have developed solid language skills and greater control over their behavior. Thanks to the practice they've had with boundaries, they're more likely to act carefully. At this stage, they're ready to take on some responsibility for themselves. This is crucial as they prepare for the start of their school life, where all the lessons they've learned will help them navigate the dynamic school environment and keep themselves safe within the boundaries of a new space.

Remember, the process won't always be linear. There will be easier days, and there will be days that feel like a constant push and pull. Some days your child may want to be close to you, while other times they'll prefer to do things on their own. It's natural for children to gradually spend more time away from their parents as they grow, working toward the independence they'll need during the preschool years when they can manage being away for several hours at a time.

Putting It into Practice To start building physical independence, I encourage you to pick an activity or skill you want to work on with your child and put it into practice. You could choose a craft project, a new skill like throwing a ball, or a daily task, such as the ones mentioned earlier—transitioning from a bottle to a cup or using a spoon to feed themselves.

Let your child try and fail as many times as they need until they master the task, but always acknowledge their progress. Remember, this will take time. Let your child move at their own pace, and be patient and supportive as you guide them through the process.

Let's move on to the next section, where I'll cover everything you need to know about when and how to teach your child to use the bathroom independently.

Lesson 3

The Potty Training Process

As I mentioned earlier, potty training is one of the topics that causes parents the most concern. This process is closely tied to both physical development and a child's sense of self-control and self-esteem. With that in mind, each child will go through this stage when they are ready.

On average, children begin to develop awareness of their bodily functions between 18 and 24 months. This is typically when they become conscious of the need to urinate or have a bowel movement. However, while this provides a general timeline, it's important to remember that every child is unique and develops at their own pace. Comparing one child's progress to another's can be both unnecessary and, in some cases, harmful.

There are many misconceptions surrounding the "right" time to stop using diapers. One common belief is that if a child becomes potty trained early, they're more advanced, or if they take longer, something is wrong. This simply isn't true. Many parents mistakenly think age alone should dictate when their child should start using the potty.

The Importance of Patience and Support

Challenges can also arise in families with multiple children. Parents may compare siblings, creating pressure. For example, if their first child stopped using diapers at 20 months, their second at 19, but their youngest isn't showing signs of readiness by 24 months, the youngest may feel pressure if the parents start to push too hard.

Let me be clear: your child will learn to use the toilet when they are ready, and this is not something you can rush. What you can do is support your child as they learn to control their body. Here are a few things to keep in mind during this process.

First, trust your child. They will give you the signs that they are ready. There are specific indicators that suggest a child is prepared for potty training. To make the process smoother and more pleasant for everyone, it's best to wait until most—or ideally, all—

of these indicators are present. This will increase the likelihood of success and reduce stress for both your child and you.

Signs of Readiness

The readiness indicators fall into three categories: physical, language, and psychosocial.

- **Physical readiness** means that your child has gained a certain level of control over their body. The most important aspect here is control of the sphincter muscles, which allow them to retain or release urine or feces. This requires a level of muscular and nervous system maturity. A good sign that they're physically ready is if they can walk without difficulty and have good coordination. Additionally, your child should be aware of how their body feels when wearing a diaper. If they aren't bothered by a dirty diaper, they won't understand the need to use the potty.

  Look for signs such as hiding when they need to poop or asking you to change their diaper when it's wet or dirty. These behaviors suggest they're becoming aware of their bodily sensations and starting to associate them with controlling their body.

- **Language readiness** is about whether your child can understand simple instructions and express their own needs or desires—both of which are crucial for potty training. The ability to follow directions shows that they can control their impulses and move their body when prompted. The ability to express their needs allows them to let you know when they need help using the toilet.

  Language skills are also essential for explaining the potty training process to your child and for them to talk about what they're feeling in their body. It's important to verbally acknowledge their attempts and successes as they learn to control their bodily functions.

- **Psychosocial readiness** involves your child's ability to understand their daily routines and anticipate events. This is more complex, as it means they recognize when using the toilet fits into their day. For instance, encouraging them to use the potty right after waking up or before bed can help them connect their bodily sensations with other daily activities, making potty training feel like a natural part of their routine.

  Another important psychosocial factor is whether your child can pause an activity without becoming upset or stressed. If they can't do this, they may struggle to stop what they're doing to use the bathroom. For this reason, it's best to wait until your child has matured emotionally before starting potty training.

It's also worth noting that potty training should be avoided during stressful periods in your child's life. Stress or major changes—such as moving, the arrival of a new sibling, or illness—can cause physical or emotional regression. Even if all the readiness signs are present, it's better to wait until your child's routine has stabilized before starting potty training. Be sure to recheck the readiness indicators before beginning.

Maintaining a Positive Approach

As with other milestones, it's essential to provide positive reinforcement to make potty training a good experience. Accidents will happen during the process, so it's crucial to maintain a warm, loving attitude that helps your child overcome setbacks and stay motivated to continue gaining control over their body.

Avoid making your child feel ashamed or upset. The goal is to ensure they feel confident to keep trying. Remember, potty training is just one of many skills they're learning, and young children are going through a lot of changes at once.

That said, don't overdo the praise either. Positive reinforcement doesn't mean throwing a party every time they use the potty. If you make too big of a deal out of it, your child might start using potty time to seek attention. It's best to treat it like any other routine activity—an important but ordinary part of their day.

Monitoring the Signs

Going back to the readiness indicators, the most important thing is consistency. It's not enough for the signs to appear just for a day or two. In order to feel confident that your child's nervous system and muscles are developed enough for proper potty control, the indicators must be present regularly.

Once your child consistently shows most or all of the readiness indicators, you can move forward with the next steps to help them transition out of diapers.

A helpful pre-training step is to let your child observe others using the toilet. Talk to them about potty training as something you'll work on together. When you notice them having a bowel movement, mention it to increase their awareness. You can also introduce a potty or a toilet seat insert. Finally, encourage your child to tell you when they feel the need to use the bathroom.

Step-by-Step Potty Training

Step 1 – Bowel Control

Here are the steps for bowel control training:

1. When your child has a bowel movement in their diaper, take them to the toilet and flush the stool together so they start to associate using the toilet with the process.

2. If your child has a regular bowel movement schedule, bring them to the potty at those times. If not, watch for signs like grunting or postures that suggest they're about to go and take them to the potty.

3. Once seated, let them stay for a short while, but avoid keeping them there too long to prevent frustration or power struggles.

4. Don't distract them with toys or books—potty time should be about focusing on their body and the task at hand.

5. If your child doesn't succeed, reevaluate the readiness indicators and restart the pre-training process.

Step 2 – Daytime Bladder Control

Next, focus on daytime bladder control:

1. Bladder control usually comes after bowel control, as the signals are less intense.

2. Watch for longer periods without urination, which indicates that their bladder is growing.

3. Dress your child in clothes that are easy to pull up and down.

4. Bring them to the potty before and after meals, naps, and playtime to incorporate it into their routine.

Step 3 – Nighttime Bladder Control

Finally, nighttime bladder control:

1. Nighttime control may not develop until after age 3.

2. Your child's bladder should be able to hold at least 330 mL (12 fl.oz.), which should allow them to stay dry through the night.

3. Avoid waking them up to use the bathroom—let them gain control at their own pace.

4. Take them to the bathroom as soon as they wake up, whether they're wet or dry. This helps reinforce the routine.

5. Don't rush nighttime potty training; pressuring them will only discourage or upset them.

6. Limit the use of nighttime pull-ups, as they can prolong the process.

Remember, potty training is a gradual process that requires all the readiness signs to be in place. First, your child will gain bowel control, then daytime bladder control, and finally nighttime bladder control. Focus on each step instead of expecting to ditch diapers overnight.

Putting It into Practice

For this lesson, observe and track the readiness indicators I've discussed over the course of a week to determine whether your child is prepared to begin potty training.

If only one or two indicators appear, that means they're not ready yet. The signs need to be consistent over a longer period. The best way to monitor this is to keep a record. This will help you identify the right time to start potty training. Ideally, your child should show most, if not all, of the indicators for over a week.

And remember—trust your child!

We're almost finished with the course. But first, in the next lesson, I'll show you how to involve your child in their personal care routines.

Lesson 4

Teaching Personal Care

Young children are eager to explore the world, and this curiosity naturally fuels their desire for independence. As parents, one of the best things we can do is to channel this natural drive into learning personal care skills.

Kids get excited about the chance to do things on their own, but it's important to recognize that if we're too critical of their efforts or dismiss their attempts to take charge, they might get discouraged and lose interest in these tasks. That's the last thing we want, right? Remember, your child is following their natural instincts—it's your role to guide their behavior with rules and boundaries they can understand.

You can begin by encouraging your child to take part in daily activities like getting dressed, having a bath, brushing their teeth, combing their hair, and feeding themselves.

Creating a Shared Routine

One way to encourage your child to take part in personal care activities is by making it a shared routine. For example, if you're giving your child a bath and they want to wash themselves, let them give it a try. After they're done, praise their effort and then let them know it's your turn to finish the job. This way, you honor their natural desire to take care of themselves without creating a power struggle. At the same time, you're teaching them about shared responsibility. They begin to understand that while they have the right to care for themselves, it's also your role as a parent to help care for them.

You can use the same approach for brushing teeth: have your child brush first, then you can follow up to ensure it's done properly.

Encouraging Cooperation

Clear, specific instructions are key when teaching personal care. It's essential to set boundaries and explain the process. Think of it as creating a "contract" between parent and child, where both sides understand what's going to happen. This approach prevents the situation from turning into a power struggle.

If the process becomes part of a daily routine, the child will know to expect parental involvement and won't feel the need to resist. Routine provides comfort and consistency for children, and when parents are reliable in their approach, it reassures them.

Another helpful technique is giving your child a choice between two necessary tasks, such as "Do you want to brush your teeth first, or put on your pajamas?" This method not only helps avoid conflict but also gives your child a sense of control and motivates them to do their best. It allows them to feel in charge of their body because they're choosing what happens next. Ultimately, the order doesn't matter as long as the personal care tasks are completed.

Offering choices fosters cooperation and self-control. It also reduces the chance of your child refusing to comply. Instead, you're giving them options that encourage independence, and you can praise them for completing both tasks well.

Choosing the Right Clothes

When it comes to getting dressed, it's important you select clothing that's appropriate for your child's level of independence. Choose clothes that are easy to put on and take off. Young children, for example, won't yet have the dexterity needed to fasten buttons or tie laces, so opt for elastic-waist pants and pull-over shirts. As they get older, around preschool age, they'll develop the ability to manage buttons and zippers, so you can gradually introduce more complex clothing.

This is also why many schools require uniforms that are easy for children to manage, especially when using the bathroom. Uniforms minimize the struggle with fasteners and buttons and help with everyday messes that are bound to happen.

There will, of course, be times when more formal clothing is necessary, like for a party or special occasions. However, for day-to-day activities, your child needs practical, easy-to-wear clothes that are also comfortable and suitable for their lifestyle. And sometimes, you can even let them choose their own outfit.

Fostering Independence Through Choice

One effective way to help your child become more independent is to prepare complete outfits ahead of time, leaving them out so your child can choose which one they'd like to wear. This gives them some autonomy without the confusion of trying to match their own clothes. After they've made their choice, you can either approve their selection or help them adjust as needed.

By offering your child tasks that match their developmental abilities, you'll help them feel more confident and willing to take on new personal care responsibilities. Allowing them to participate in their own care from an early age is one of the best ways to raise an independent child. Over time, they'll learn to care for themselves, while still sharing some of that responsibility with you.

Introducing personal care gradually, starting as early as the first year of life, helps your child get used to these tasks. By age two, most children can take part in daily personal care activities with your guidance. This sense of self-control and confidence will lay the groundwork for future skills, like learning in school or trying new challenges. Involving your child in their personal care routine at a young age helps them understand their ability to manage their world.

Putting It into Practice

For this exercise, choose one personal care task that your child can start participating in. If they're old enough, have them try dressing themselves or brushing their teeth while you guide them. If they get messy while eating, have them help wash their face afterward.

At bedtime, encourage them to undress and put on the pajamas you've laid out for them. If you usually give them a bath at night, let them take a more active role in the process.

It's important to introduce these tasks one at a time. Stick with one task for a few weeks before adding another to the routine—unless your child shows interest in doing more. The key is to pay attention to what your child is ready for and let them progress at their own pace.

Conclusion

Wonderful! We've reached the end. Now you have the tools to set appropriate boundaries while guiding your child toward greater independence each day.

As humans, we are hardwired from our DNA to develop skills and abilities. This isn't something exceptional or rare. As parents, the best we can do is support our children in this natural process, following their lead in terms of timing and pace.

During the first year, your little one will rely on you for almost everything, but you'll soon notice them trying to do a few things on their own, and this interest will grow as they get older. The key is to guide them, finding a balance between their need for dependence and their growing desire for autonomy.

It takes time for every child to reach this balance. Patience and objectivity are essential to setting realistic expectations while helping your child develop new skills successfully. There's no need to rush or hold them back; simply be present and watch for their changes, always ready to guide them.

One of the core aims of Proactive Parenting is to help you anticipate behaviors. It's not about solving every problem for them or forbidding certain actions—it's about understanding the developmental stages your child is going through and using that knowledge to observe their progress, adjusting boundaries as needed.

Boundaries Are the Foundation for Freedom

Ultimately, this is how children learn to manage themselves in a controlled way. The boundaries you set for your child during their early years will serve as the foundation for their future freedom. Real freedom requires both self-control and confidence. The goal of parenting is to protect and guide our children so they can become fully capable members of society, able to care for themselves as well as those around them.

In recent years, I've noticed that some parents seem to want to extend the experience of having a young child, perhaps to savor this phase a little longer. However, this can hinder the child's development. Sometimes, this happens due to impatience or the lack of time parents have to match the pace set by their child.

We must support our children at every stage and encourage their independence. How do you think you'll feel when you see your child managing basic personal care tasks on their own? You'll have more time to focus on other things, and your child will feel a sense of pride and accomplishment in taking care of themselves. Fostering this confidence is essential for their growth. Over time, both you and your child will see the benefits and be grateful for the effort. Remember, the work you put in today will shape the teenager and the adult they become in the future.

Some Final Reminders

Each age and stage comes with different challenges and risks, all tied to your child's developmental abilities. You'll need to make adjustments throughout their growth process.

There are boundaries that are non-negotiable. It's crucial to make sure your child understands these, using clear instructions, consistent actions, and repetition.

Your child's ability to control their own body will depend on your trust in how they're navigating these new experiences. Never pressure them—encourage their interest in new tasks and celebrate their successes.

If you enjoyed this course, you might also like *The Proven Method for Getting Your Kid to Eat, Sleep & Play Happily*, available on my website and through all major audio platforms. In that course, I offer tips to develop healthy sleep and eating habits, and how to encourage screen-free play.

Remember, there's no such thing as perfect parenting, and your children aren't expected to be perfect either. Sometimes you'll both make mistakes, and that's okay. What's important is that you're doing your best. The fact that you're here, learning more about your child's development, shows that you're on the right track. With your guidance, they'll gain the independence they need. Congratulations!

Disponible como audio curso en:

- Audiobooks.com
- Audible
- Chirp
- Everand (Scribd)
- Google Play
- Hoopla
- Kobo
- Libro.fm
- NOOK Audiobooks
- Spotify (sólo en USA, UK y AUS)
- Storytel

www.ingramcontent.com/pod-product-compliance
Lightning Source LLC
LaVergne TN
LVHW010505160826
845677LV00012B/2676
* 9 7 8 8 4 1 2 9 2 7 1 3 9 *